CANADIAN
POSTAL WORKERS

With thanks to Deby Martin
at Canada Post.

P.B. and K.L.

Kids Can Press Ltd. acknowledges with appreciation the assistance of the Canada Council and the Ontario Arts Council in the production of this book.

CANADIAN CATALOGUING IN PUBLICATION DATA

Bourgeois, Paulette
Canadian postal workers

(In my neighbourhood)
ISBN 1-55074-058-X (bound) ISBN 1-55074-135-7 (pbk.)

1. Postal service – Canada – Juvenile literature.
2. Postal service   Canada – Employees – Juvenile literature. I. LaFave, Kim. II. Title.
III. Series: Bourgeois, Paulette. In my neighbourhood.

HE6655.B68 1992   j383'.4971   C91-095197-7

Kids Can Press Ltd.
29 Birch Avenue
Toronto, Ontario, Canada
M4V 1E2

Designed by N.R. Jackson
Typeset by Cybergraphics Co. Inc.
Printed and bound in Hong Kong by Everbest Co., Ltd.

PA 93 0 9 8 7 6 5 4 3 2 1

CANADIAN POSTAL WORKERS

In My Neighbourhood

Paulette Bourgeois

Kim LaFave

KIDS CAN PRESS LTD.
Toronto

"Oh, no!" says Gordon. "Grandma's birthday is only four days away and I haven't sent a card."

Gordon chooses his very best paper and draws a picture of rainbows and balloons. He writes a special message and puts the card in an envelope.

He crosses his fingers. "I hope she gets this in time."

The card must travel all the way across the country.

Gordon writes Grandma's address and his address on the front of the envelope. He checks the postal code twice — mail moves faster when the address is correct. Then he walks to the post office to buy a stamp.

The money for the stamp pays for the mail to travel from one place to another. When people send special mail, such as big parcels or rush mail, they pay more money to the post office for the extra service.

Gordon looks at all the stamps and chooses very carefully. He licks the glue on the back of the stamp and sticks it on before he slides his card into the mailbox.

Once a day, a driver opens the mailbox and puts the envelopes into a big bag. Special mail goes in special bags that the postmaster gives the driver. The driver collects mail along the route and takes it to a letter-processing centre in the closest big city.

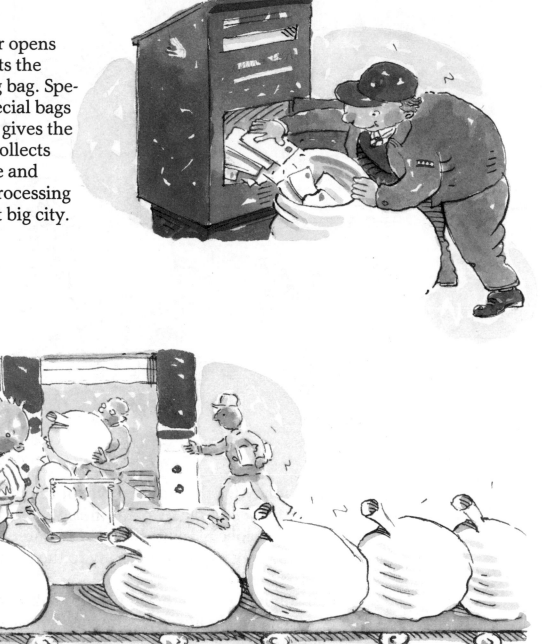

There, all the bags from all the drivers are dumped onto a conveyor belt. When the bags are opened, there are letters, cards and parcels going all over the world. Postal workers sort out special mail, parcels and letters that are too big or too small for the machines.

A machine called a culler-facer-canceller does three jobs in one. Just in case the human sorters missed an odd-sized envelope, the machine spits out all the mail that won't fit. Then it makes sure that all the fronts of the envelopes are facing the same direction.

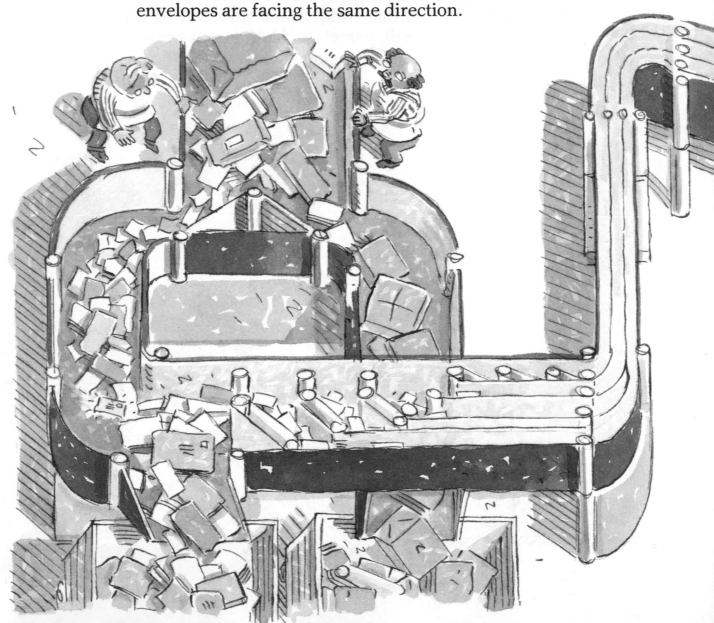

Next, the machine cancels the stamps by making a squiggly mark on them. A cancelled stamp cannot be used again. Stamps are like tickets — they're good for only one trip!

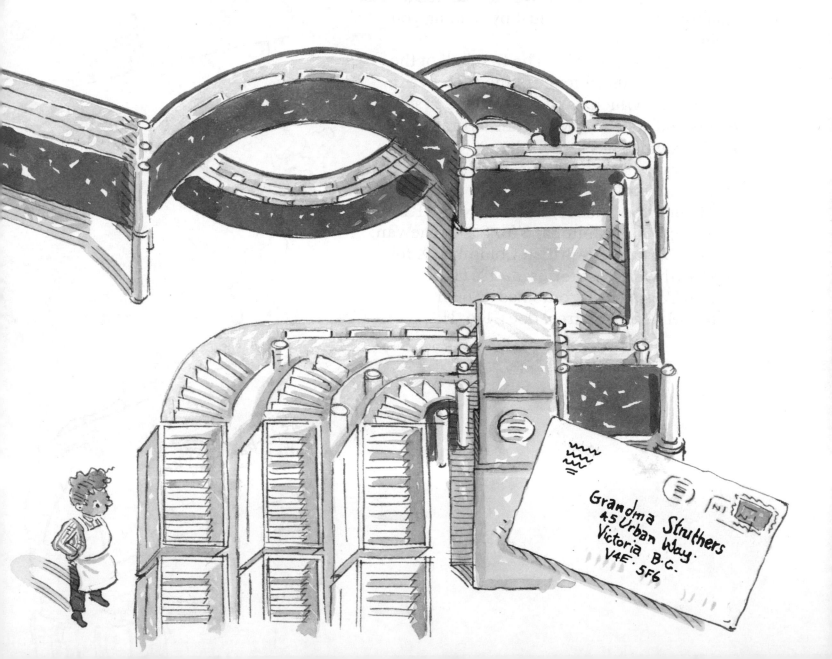

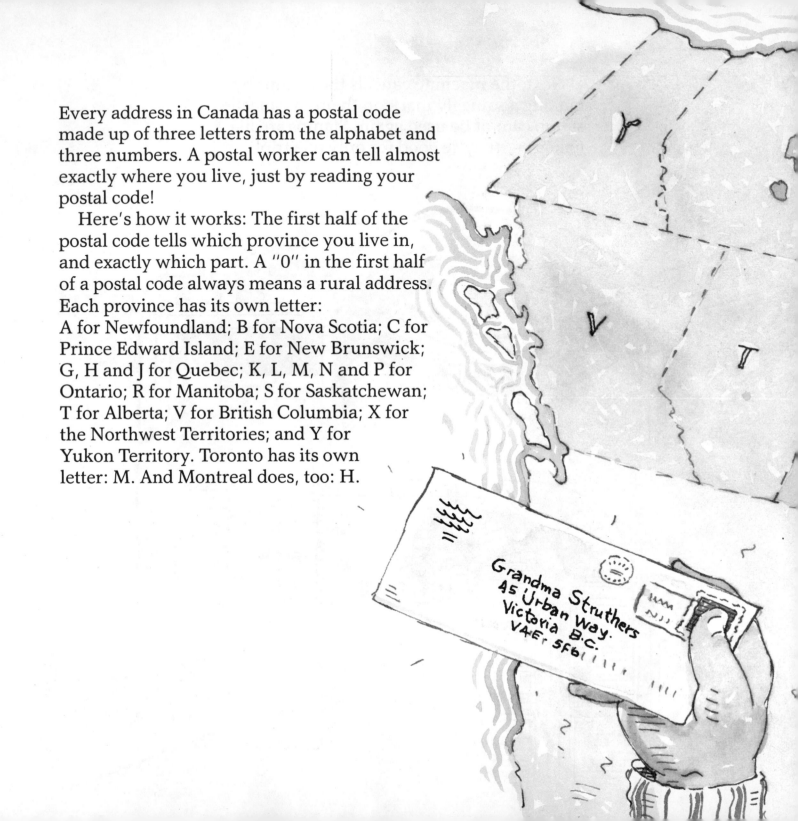

Every address in Canada has a postal code made up of three letters from the alphabet and three numbers. A postal worker can tell almost exactly where you live, just by reading your postal code!

Here's how it works: The first half of the postal code tells which province you live in, and exactly which part. A "0" in the first half of a postal code always means a rural address. Each province has its own letter:
A for Newfoundland; B for Nova Scotia; C for Prince Edward Island; E for New Brunswick; G, H and J for Quebec; K, L, M, N and P for Ontario; R for Manitoba; S for Saskatchewan; T for Alberta; V for British Columbia; X for the Northwest Territories; and Y for Yukon Territory. Toronto has its own letter: M. And Montreal does, too: H.

Grandma Struthers
45 Urban Way.
Victoria B.C.
V4Er 5F6

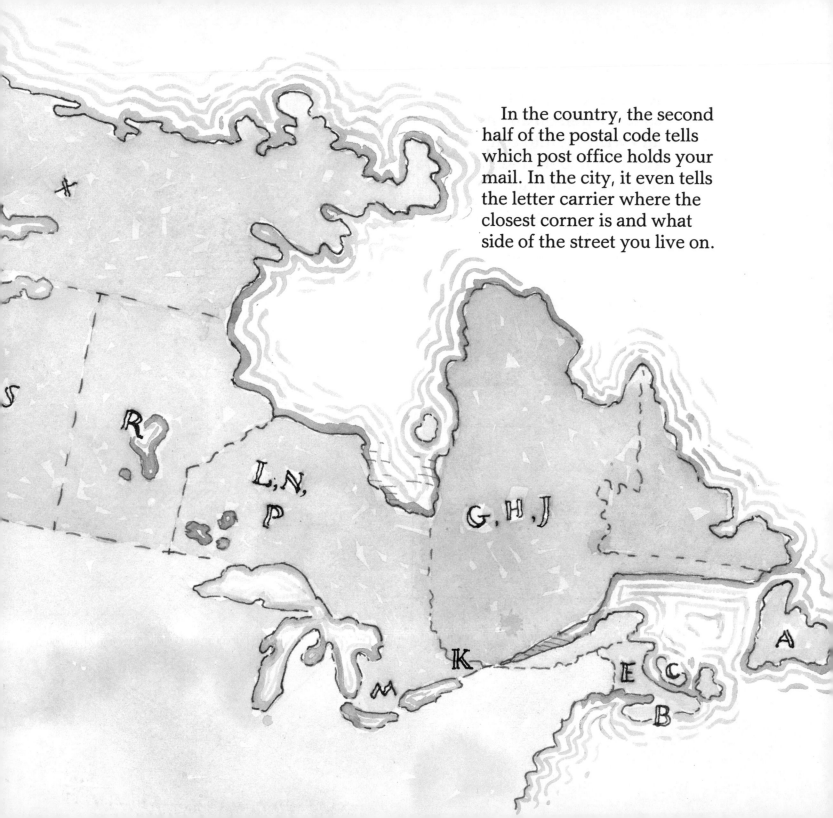

In the country, the second half of the postal code tells which post office holds your mail. In the city, it even tells the letter carrier where the closest corner is and what side of the street you live on.

A computer reads the postal
code written on an envelope
and writes it into computer lan-
guage that looks like yellow bars
on envelope fronts.

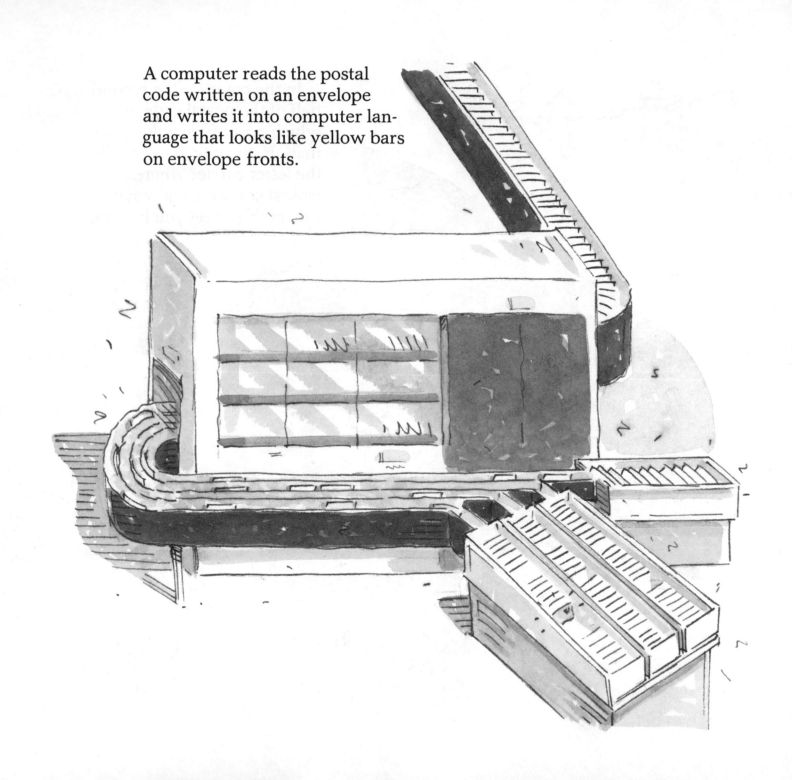

Letters whiz through a sorting machine that
reads the computerized postal codes and sorts
the envelopes onto different conveyor belts.
Gordon's letter moves along the belt until it
drops into a bag marked Victoria. The mail
bags travel mostly by truck and by plane.

The card from Gordon has travelled night and day to the postal station near his Grandma's.

It is still cold, dark and early when Grandma's letter carrier gets to work. A postal worker has already sorted the mail into routes and put it into big, heavy bags.

The letter carrier picks up her satchel and sorts her mail into slots that are marked by street and building numbers. "Whew!" she says. "Must be a lot of birthdays coming up."

There's too much mail for the letter carrier to take all at once. She puts as much mail as she can carry into her satchel. The rest she puts into bags that will be taken by a driver to locked corner boxes on her route. The letter carriers drag their bags to the waiting trucks. "Hurry, hurry," the drivers shout.

Letter carriers have to be ready for snow, sleet, sun, rain.

Full bags can weigh up to 17 kilograms (35 pounds) each

Dark running shoes or boots

Needs new shoes every couple of months

SPRING

SUMMER

Shoulder flashes on each arm

Must be physically fit

AUTUMN   WINTER

The letter carrier walks fast on her route. She steps around garbage cans, marches up steps and slides the mail into mail slots. She watches out for ice in the winter. And she hopes owners of angry dogs will keep them leashed and out of her way.

Letter carriers deliver the mail, they do not read it — not even funny postcards from far away. But they do care who collects their mail and who doesn't. Some postal workers are community watchdogs. They know the elderly people on their route.

When their mail is not collected, the postal worker calls a special phone number to report something suspicious. Perhaps the person fell and can't get up. A relative or friend is sent to check. Postal workers save lives this way.

By the time the letter carrier reaches her corner box, called a relay box, her satchel is empty. She uses a key to spring the lock open. She fills her shoulder bag again. "What a gorgeous yellow envelope," she says.

Grandma gets a big smile on her face when she opens her mailbox. There are cards from all over Canada and the world. "Goodness, something from Gordon. His card is early. My birthday isn't until tomorrow."

Grandma tapes Gordon's card on her fridge. She loves the card, but she loves the stamp on the envelope, too. Grandma is a stamp collector. She takes out a large leather binder and adds Gordon's birthday stamp to her collection.

On her other mail, there are stamps from Canada, Japan, Peru and Greece. She already knows what she will send Gordon for his birthday: a card made of special paper with a dozen stamps from a dozen countries tucked inside an envelope.

Grandma seals her envelope
and addresses it carefully.

She puts the stamp here.

She puts her address on the top left corner
of the envelope like this:

MRS A STRUTHERS
45 URBAN WAY
VICTORIA BC V4E 5F6

She puts Gordon's address in the centre of
the envelope like this:

GORDON NORMAN
2 GULLS WAY
GO BY CHANCE NF A0B 2C3

Gordon checks his community mailbox every day.
Soon it will be his birthday, and Grandma always
sends him a big fat envelope with something special
tucked inside.